I0618056

MENTAL ILLNESS

John Ruonavaara

UnMask

Copyright 2023 by John Ruonavaara

All rights reserved. This book or any portion thereof may not be reproduced or used in any manner whatsoever without the express written permission of the publisher except for the use of brief quotation in a book review.

ISBN: 978-1-961416-06-2 (sc)
ISBN: 978-1-961416-07-9 (hc)
ISBN: 978-1-961416-08-6 (ebk)

CONTENTS

PREFACE

The idea and inspiration behind this book on mental health was written with the intent to further help educate the plot and many variables of an individual challenged, that may have a like transparency and or similar traits that are parallel in experience.

I truly think the more we are aware and are familiar with symptoms, we can avoid and possibly prevent symptoms from reoccurring.

I think it is important while reading this book, is to understand outside of those who are challenged with mental health issues, that there is,a medical team at large.

Not all physical labor can be equivalent to someone who may be experiencing extreme levels of Mental Health conditions especially in and out of episodes.

The courage it took to write this book, its only key factors that have matters of relevance and I felt the need to be addressed.

I want to instruct to those who may be suffering with mental health conditions, that before anything else your honesty with your medical team is extremely important, we do not want to fall prey to the creativity of avoiding details, our strength comes when we learn to address issues.

The one and true desire that I would want for publication is first and foremost to those, that may have mental health challenges, that I had every intention to provide our readers a way to better understand just how difficult it can be. In ways I feel like a brother in arms and I truly can empathize with this depth.

SUMMARY

We are going to try to do the most comprehensive interview, based on the life and experiences and its magnitude of one suffering, and the challenges, in order to give our readers an open window to the Meticulous Interiors of someone who has went through a PROLONGED Mental Health Recovery.

We want to educate our readers on any early development foreseen in youth that may have been a contributing factor to diagnosis later on.

We also want to educate on an entire scope on the many variables of what one might experience when and if with the crisis of a mental health breakdown.

It is the intention to draw awareness to either Community Support team's family or friends, should we know someone who may be struggling with like symptoms, that this model would help further educate how we as individuals might be able to help even in worst-case scenarios.

We would also like to bring insight to what were the working components in the success, in order to achieve recovery and its benefits.

Earliest Memories

Could you bring us through some of your earliest memories of your youth, that might have been apparent of a possible lurking mental health concern that later could have potential influenced and maybe would have possibly helped define your diagnosis?

ANSWER

I was diagnosed with bipolar a week before my 18th birthday.

In answer to your question I had a very upsetting and sporadic history starting from such a young age.

I'm going to take some time to explain this because I think it's important.

I was stubborn and strong headed, I think being strong willed is good in ways, although also has its disadvantages as far as adapting and learning from experiences that would give a better susceptibility to learn, listen, and achieve.

I guess it shows in some of my upbringing, this inconsistency in my chemistry and its sporadic way of expressing itself, for example around 12 years old chasing my brothers and sisters in rage with a knife, basically cooping them in the upstairs.

My frustrations in life and how I dealt with issues at that time was only justified through acts of self-thought bravery and twisted ideology's. I was very critical minded and those ideologies as much of an influence as they might have been, I remained demanding of respect.

My mindset grew stronger with ignorance. My dad could not wrap his mind around what to do with me. In many cases almost given him several heart attacks. It was awkward, I guess in a few ways because I lacked empathy.

My idea was that people made me the problem and I became very stubborn because of that. It was in disarray and a bit uncomfortable and I always had something to say to counter react their decisions on issues.

My headstrong reaction with my dad would make him collapse on the couch almost hyperventilating, holding his chest saying "what am I going to do with you".

I was not very well accepting of others and their opinions, but rather my Relentless determination to pursue the ideas that I valued as an individual. I still remember vividly all the different characters of these environments.

At the age of 14 one of my friends pinned me to the ground and I end up getting up and when I did eventually find what I wanted for a weapon I chased after him halfway down the block with a hatchet. Fortunately, nothing physically ever happened in these situations, other than marking my territory I guess.

Because of the confusion of understanding me and I saw that it was obvious within my family and friends, I would use experiences like this to experiment the consequences or levels of respect in order to benefit from.

It was kind of like a self-inflicting science experiment in a way. I think this fueling character inside me especially with a temperament and chaotic rationale drew a lot of different conclusions.

It continued to escalate my experiences and frustrations, the only time I was introduced of possibly having a mental health illness, was on the eve of my diagnosis.

One of the most astounding observations Within Myself from youth was, I really felt like I was paying more attention to life than those around me. This feeling never really ever went away even while my chemistry was being medically induced. I have always felt things deeply.

On the outside my character was similar to a Roaring lion deep within me I was a humble boy, compassionate to those less fortunate, I guess I still in some ways feel like these characters I think only strengthened in me over time.

As a youth in school I had developed an obvious learning disability which in turn, required special needs.

As a student in a learning disability class separated from those that were not required for special needs, I observed.

Inside my classroom and on the playground, I saw my classmate's characters, low income kids, empty to feel or develop caring friends, and from the outside they were easy prey to distinguish their poverty, whether it was in education, image, social interactions or self-worth.

Through this experience I developed a natural compassion and in ways Protected Their poverty-stricken realities.

It seemed like the rest of the world went on while I studied these segregation characteristics.

••

Q.   **These outbursts and frustrations did they release themselves fairly short, or is this something that maybe continued ongoing for a while?**

A.   I think the way I Justified my anger was suit for the occasion and usually I would return back to a more reserved State of Mind, although my reasoning continued to be very sporadic and definitely was a DISTINGUISHED level of fury.

Q.   **You mentioned your experience felt awkward can you maybe give us an idea for why you may have chosen that word to describe your frustrations with that event?**

A.   To be honest as a kid and in my frustration, I felt since he was the dad he was supposed to know what to do and I guess that's when I began to conclude I was a bundle.

Q. **How well accepting where you to be placed in a learning disability classroom?**

A. My first impression was that I was in a classroom with a bunch of other rebels in some cases, they all invited me and I got to be friends with them, a little bit more my style. Although some of them eventually went to another school. But to answer your question I guess I got some more dream time in, I thought that was pretty cool.

Although I must say as much as the conveniences, there was reverse effects, I wasn't where I wanted to be. My attitude towards life because of unsettling home life, was that I don't care anymore, but I'm going to pay attention.

"SOME OF THE BEST STEPS
ARE THE EARLIEST ONES"
John Ruonavaara

Creativity Inspirations Youth

How about creativity as a youth, was there moments that you may have felt inspired?

ANSWER

Actually yes, probably one of the most memorable experiences with creativity and the feeling of being inspired was at the age of 15 working for summer youth program for the local elementary school in my hometown.

I remember distinctively the energy and stimulation that was in a way charging my chemistry.

I would be semi-focusing on my work, at that time I was cleaning kid's desktops and chairs, all I remember is this stirring creativity in a way of feeling extremely compassionate, as if I was being introduced to a higher calling.

It was as if being plugged into electrical outlet, I would be thinking about a situation or certain characters in my life, as far as people I may have met and in this experience, I would feel so energized or powered with compassion.

I think the most fascinating part of this experience was that I was experiencing all these emotions and inspiration and my boss and working partner had no idea this was happening.

I could feel the purity and compassion as if I was talking to a bigger crowd, this left quite an impression on me.

One of the biggest thunderstorms I've ever seen hit this area came during this experience and moved in at 45 miles an hour and super high winds it went from blue calm, to BLACK!

This thunderstorm took off the roof cap of the elementary school tossing it into pieces on the ground.

The significance of this experience with Creativity Flow was definitely remembered, in part, because of this storm.

••

Q. **What was the nature of your conversation with this bigger crowd?**

A. I was encouraging people, I felt like my compassion exceeded a new level outside of what I've ever heard in my church community or from family. That feeling and experience never left me.

Q. **Would you say that you were communicating with an energy or higher power?**

A. It definitely made a big impact on me, I think in a way it was yes, both.

"VISIONARY CREATIVITIES IN YOUTH ARE THE GENERATING FORCE TO BRIGHT FUTURES"
John Ruonavaara

QUESTION:

Triggers

As the growing years of your teens was there anything else that may have altered or heightened your awareness that may have played into the chemistry of your diagnosis?

ANSWER

Early teens I experimented with the same-sex curiosity, and it had some unexpected consequences, my upbringing as far my church community was known for their rigidity and polarizing demeans, which in those days seemed more so, having to said that, word leaked about the experience, and if my mind was not already peeked this raised the roof to a whole new level of concern.

What was once an unavoidable curiosity turned into the Sensory Hazard and massive leaps of assumption, always super aware.

I developed a personal protection against the idea that I personally did not become the laughing stock of the jokes of others.

I say unavoidable because we were roughneck friends. So obviously through school and in our church community, paranoia and determination had its crippling effects.

Overtime I generated a super-conscious awareness on high alert at all times, especially when I conspired and sensed attacks.

This definitely changed the dynamic since it was an invisible force and war I was up against.

I would be sitting in class and I get the possible hint that the teacher is trying to maybe persuade a message that was not necessarily obvious to the rest of the class.

I thought it was designed for a pinpoint assumption and an attack on me.

You can imagine how on the edge of the seat at any given circumstance.

The reality of this experience, you can't explain to anyone, and you can't talk about those that may unintentionally be killing you inside.

I was so overly concerned about this matter I truly felt helpless.

My intuitive sense and psychological aspect as far as picking up on information then feeling the dire need to sort was exhausting.

In a way because of the humiliation, I was directly over-committed to have a girlfriend.

This experience I think was the pivoting point to a much larger invisible exercise, that ultimately dictated the entire psych.

I am very much aware of the construct and interior battles that send conflicting messages.

In ways this experience can actually consume the identity and its ability to influence every thought.

This definitely had an impact on the way I was challenged and how ultimately increased part of the chemistry before diagnosis.

· ·

Q. You must have thought that quite a few people were workingagainst you?

A. Actually yes lots of my thoughts polarized and conspired bits of nothing. I think what made it all the more reason to have a heightened influence to be polarized, is the very culture and beliefs we naturally inquire to, be it religious affiliated or simply our separation gaps of good and bad.

Q. Do you feel like your friends felt the same way?

A. Yes and no we didn't talk about it much.

Q. If you could change one thing about this experience what would that be?

A. Everyone has weaknesses growing up and even into adult life, I think as a whole we need to help educate on how to deal with stress at any level.

Q. How do you feel about others that may support this type of lifestyle?

A. My model supports authenticity's.

Q. What was the message to you inside this experience that you benefited the most from?

A. My predictions for what I assumed only Made Me Stronger and more Equipped.

"JUST BECAUSE THERE'S ROOM FOR
DOUBT DON'T GET COMFORTABLE"
John Ruonavaara

QUESTION:

First Girlfriend

When were you active in what may have been your first RELATIONSHIP?

ANSWER

I was 16 years old, I had my first car then, honestly, I felt like I was on top of the world but also consequently because of my chemistry and super awareness to the surroundings I became very critical of myself.

I was really excited about this relationship and I think I overlooked a lot of stuff I guess that's the nature of young love.

I've became over-committed way too fast, because I was so hung up on this relationship I had no reserve plan should the relationship not eventually work out.

The gnawing reminder of my past continued to press an evaluated unnecessary level of seriousness.

The dating period was not long until she eventually called it off.

I was caught up with the idea that if you prayed and were sincere everything would work out.

When this breakup came, it was a feeling of severe grief and betrayal.

Often times people that are suffering or have death or losses in their life it can affect their chemistry and I think that was the turning point.

Almost a year later I was diagnosed with bipolar inside the psychiatric treatment Center in Marquette General Hospital.

The reason why I feel this was a turning point is immediately after this event I started a more chaotic attitude, abstract in a way.

I felt like I needed to display chaos in order to justify the feeling of Chaos.

It was the only comfort I could give myself and that weirdness went on even after the diagnosis.

I continued to show patterns of inconsistency and abstract thinking, for example laughing at things and mixing up words, in order to either draw attention or distract the obviousness.

•••

Q. Did you speculate that your girlfriend at the time may have known anything about your same-sex curiosity?

A. I don't think it played that much of a factor.

Q. Do you feel because of this experience was unable to be tangible, that it left you frustrated with the process and its acceptance with reality?

A. Exactly, and I think a lot of my processing as far as information was very determined and my expectations were much higher, for something so premature.

"MYSTERIOUS WAYS AND IT'S UNRAVELINGS"
John Ruonavaara

1st Break-Down Alert

When did others for the first time begin to notice a concern for mental health evaluation?

ANSWER

Well actually it started first with me, it was as if I was experiencing a super heightened level of awareness and being related as an Awakening, I remember going to school and having these emotions flow through me with rapid thoughts.

I remember talking to my school friends at lunch and trying to explain to them of this really big thing that is going to happen.

Basically, I was stuck on the idea that everyone was going to be experiencing this hyped reality or Awakening.

Me personally I have never heard or ever thought that there might be a psychiatric issue with the way I was thinking.

It never occurred to me that there would be such things as a diagnosis for those with manic depressive states.

I remember distinctly looking at people's faces as I would drive past them in my vehicle and thinking that a network was in control and it was affecting other people and not just me and I guess by looking at their faces whether they were sad or happy I would conclude with the idea that the network is in a figure of speech was hot-wired.

At this particular time in my life my mom and dad were on a vacation in the West Coast with other family members and my brother and his wife were basically looking after us.

I can remember the jarring sets of emotion I was going through when I would be talking in the living room that evening with my brother or other siblings.

I knew I was conveying multiple suspicions on its monstrosity and in a sense exhausting at the same time.

All of this altered chemistry was within a two-week period. I definitely at this time as it began to peak could feel the manic spins of grandiosity and emotional roller coasting.

I guess one of the main things that was kind of interesting was that it was not an alternative motive that I would be switching into for that time.

I thought this was my new life and that how strange it was, a mix between pretty pumped on myself and oh no will this keep going.

Part of what my feeling and depth was pivoting on was the idea of my spirituality at the time and significance in how I related to that spirituality.

I could imagine I guess those of old times that did not have a medical intervention that was humane and supported how they might have felt and the extension to why they would be cast out as evil spirits or possessed by alternate or dark forces.

Being in the church community at this time, as part of our leisure time, evenings we would gather at other members homes, usually part of that experience we would talk about certain questions about maybe life in general or things that was mentioned in the church and then we would talk individually about how we felt.

At this event I was definitely paying attention to all and truly preoccupied as far as fabricating on what I was going to make comment on and this was not uncommon for me at all, even throughout my history with the diagnosis always kind of prefabbing some kind of unique depth.

I remember as I was relating my answer I was definitely geared and emotionally pressured in fact having to bust out crying during part of what is explaining, definitely could not shake it at all, it was so much in my system.

I can understand what people feel like when they are being overcome with mixed psychosis or emotions that can relate to emotional either breakdowns or just difficulty getting through the day.

At this point I could recognize people were becoming more concerned by the day.

And I guess my family and others were never really educated in any way that supported the idea of possible mental health conditions.

....

Q. Can you explain why it would be difficult for someone to accept a medical intervention, in response to what this feeling might be like?

A. First of all during this experience like this you have a superiority idea and influence as if you are being directed by God, it gets to a point that you develop a lot of confidence and ownership of this condition, and much like an alternator on a vehicle it keeps generating charge.

Because the nature of these thoughts has a sense of privacy, it makes it all the more difficult to see it as a medical condition.

Day Of Diagnosis

Can you bring us through that day that you were first being admitted to the hospital for a complete diagnosis of what you may have been struggling with?

ANSWER

It wasn't until early evening in the late part of February 1997 that my family really began to look on the issue to find a resolution and began to be aware that this is something that needs attention soon.

My parents were not scheduled to be home yet from their vacation but because of the crisis they were able to hit an early flight, although by that time I was already admitted.

That night I remember my brothers and sisters making arrangements to visit the church minister.

I end up being brought over there by my sister-in-law.

It's amazing to me to actually think back now, I remember waiting for such a long time in the living room while my sister-in-law spend time upstairs talking to him, the details of that evening are still very crystal clear.

One of my sisters came shortly after and joined where they were talking, while I continue to sit in the living room.

I guess my thought at that time was like, good luck if you going to try to fix whatever was happening, I knew it was a monster inside of me.

It was a very awkward experience after getting to talk with all of them together. I went from owning my mania, to speculating and unresolved.

The council and decision were to seek emergency room visit to see about balance and chemistry, they explained a little bit about it in the meeting but it did not make sense to me too much.

We eventually made it to the emergency room, little did I know that I was going to be seeing a lot of this for the next 20 years as far as visiting emergency rooms for the crisis of mental health.

Regardless, the emergency room doctor said he was requesting a specialist to come and have a visit with me.

While I was waiting I must have missed the conversation outside of the emergency room door because when my sister came in she said that you might have bipolar or something like that and that many famous people have had what you are experiencing and she was naming off a several of them.

So, I guess I wasn't too disappointed, after the visiting the specialist and honestly answering all his questions it wasn't too long after that that they were requesting a visit to Marquette General Hospital child unit psychiatric evaluation center.

The one thing that I told my brothers on the way down to this visit at the time, was if there is a medication in order to help me think better in which they explained, I said, look out!

Probably the only light moment of the trip, I just remember my empty stare for the greater part of that transport.

At that time because it was so new to me, at the age of 17, I had the privilege to be able to have transportation through my brothers.

· ·

Q. While in the hospital for the first time and being treated for mental health evaluation what were your best and maybe worst moments of that experience?

A. My best was because I was still 17 years old I was able to be admitted into the child's unit knowing the benefits of avoiding an overstimulating adult unit.

My other better part was, I really enjoyed the food in fact I remember having roast beef with melted cheese inside of a bun definitely really good.

My most difficult part of this experience was that I had an interior conflict with myself and the reality and conditions in which I found myself in.

It felt very weird personally because I still had a lot of grandiosity, and ego fixed spirituality.

Simultaneously in this experience I was feeling a greater part of despair and made mention to one of the hospital staff about having him to go away in the name of Jesus, something I learned as a kid and he whipped his head around and said, who said that, before I could actually take it in, I was distracted, my brothers were in the window at the unit and they were just arriving to visit with me, but I did not forget that experience.

Q. **You talked about being admitted how did you feel when your parents arrived?**

A. I felt kind of absent with the emotion of spaced confusions, the introductory to Mental Health has basic elements but the psychological effects can be a bit overwhelming.

I remember my dad telling me that he has never heard of mental health or for that matter what I was being diagnosed, bipolar disorder.

They asked what I would like for supper and I think I remember ordering Wendy's.

On their return visit that evening they brought my supper and I was able to eat and visit in my room with them.

"HE CLIMBED OVER THE MOUNTAIN
AND SAW ANOTHER MOUNTAIN"
John Ruonavaara

Philosophy Of My Youth

Is there any way you would like to sum up about your youth or any general philosophy before moving on to our next question?

ANSWER

I was a pretty normal 80s child outside of what I was thinking and collecting that actually played part in my diagnosis.

We played lots of street hockey, we built forts in the woods, we had motorbikes we swam in rivers, we played cops and robbers with our bicycles behind my parents' house, we've had picnics at parks next to Lake Superior, and I guess I was kind of adventurous.

I guess to sum it up I've had good memories.

I was also a very big Dreamer I could make situations seem like Infinity, basically get lost on what I was doing.

My general philosophy had a peculiar interest and hunger with life.

* * *

Q. **As a youth did you enjoy any type of music being played at that time?**

A. Yes actually when I first started listening to music I was kind of in a way disappointed that the music had lyrics

26

when I first started listening, I liked the Acoustics in the music the best.

Three of my most popular songs while growing up in the 80s was the song Final Countdown, the Eye of the Tiger, and Madonna Open your Heart.

In fact, every one of the 13 times I would be hospitalized in a psychiatric unit I would be singing to myself The Final Countdown it always seemed to lift my spirits.

I think this is similar to the dream state I attracted as a kid.

"A CHILD WITH LITTLE BIG EYES"
John Ruonavaara

Mental Health Intro

This next question is an overview on Mental Health, how would you generalize the scope of this term?

ANSWER

Mental health is a very wide spectrum of many different challenges people may be directly diagnosed with or are familiar of someone battling or in recovery with symptoms related to issues under psychological unbalanced deficiencies.

The depth of the human mind has so many variables and levels of psychosis that continue to influence mental health facilities and the study of psychology, so this term Mental Health in collaboration is massive.

On a medical side doctors look for symptoms in order to give an educated evaluation to the traits.

· ·

Q. How do you feel about the consequence of the Mind suffering in a crisis, do you feel they will ever be able to achieve Wellness?

A. In the process of my past 21 years and experience with multiple mental health life crisis experiences, I have heard of brain cells dying when you go through an episode and have heard that you will never receive them back again.

I think it is too soon to make that decision on this theory, my theory is that just as the body receives scars and those scars actually make that part of the skin stronger, I guess in concept I feel the brain works the same way as it calluses an experience in order to give you strength for wellness however prolonged it might be, even though some people struggling may appear a bit lifeless.

I also believe in the evolutionary side of human progress, as we begin to use new tools and adapt to new medications we're all diamonds, often times outside of a struggling mind are the most beautiful heart's.

These human conditions of a mental disorder are so often capable of displaying the wrong message.

"OVER TIME PLEASE LET ME SHINE"
John Ruonavaara

A Time For ER

From your personal experience while having the diagnosis what was some of the alarming concerns from people around you or also within yourself, that would meet the needs of evaluation or ER screening?

ANSWER

I think from my own personal experience we need to take into account that my first diagnosis of having bipolar disorder basically the idea of mood swings, was not enough of a diagnosis.

There was a lot more going on inside my chemistry.

It was only revealed to my doctor in May of 2014 a new diagnosis under the condition of "bipolar schizoid-affective disorder" which has traits of schizophrenia but it's not directly related.

So many times, I remember sitting in my vehicle after getting to a location and telling myself, man, if I could only slow down my brain, it was very frustrating although I did not think there was such thing.

I could not help getting mad at people and it showed miserably.

I was trying to live life and I had all the best intentions but I could not deliver and kept having relapse in the hospital.

The majority of reasons why I would end up in the hospital was because of being misunderstood, overwhelmed, and the questionable levels of safety that was developed on issues that showed extreme levels of anger.

There are times though that the screening process if at all possible they would avoid putting you in a hospital and rather try to arrange Care through a group home nearby, usually affiliated with mental health.

....

Q. What do you think you learned most of this experience goodor bad?

A. I found out that if you stand on issues not to be afraid to hold your ground, although with good chemistry now I have a tactical way of dealing with things rather than letting them spin out of control and its related to sustain peace and try to understand.

Sometimes the best thing to do is absolutely nothing. Although if I'm provoked or I feel that my values are being overlooked in a situation I am not at all withdrawn from speaking and addressing the issue correctly.

"THE SIGNIFICANCE OF BALANCE CHEMISTRY"
John Ruonavaara

Crisis Guiding

On this next segment, what do you have to say about those who are being introduced to Mental Health whether they are being diagnosed or simply a family member by the aid of someone suffering.

ANSWER

Without a full evaluation there are many variables related to whether the person would need to be hospitalized.

If a person is seeking medical attention there is a screening process that is in place in order to justify needs for hospitalization.

Two of the most common characters that give concern for in-hospital evaluation, is if the person is either a danger to their self or others and has had Suicidal Thoughts.

If the person is noticeably unstable this experience and stigma can escalate, mainly because of the person's chemistry and incoherent psychosis.

If a person is being introduced to Mental Health it is most appropriate to first try to schedule an appointment with a mental health clinic if it is not an immediate crisis.

Certain symptoms to look for in a medical mental health condition would be lack of sleep, difficult time concentrating, having crying spells over a period of time and polarized or elevated mood.

There are also other symptoms as agitation and overly self-critical.

Looking for signs in the individual or if you are an independent such things as a loss of Interest in everyday life obligations or enjoyments.

Some may relate to obsessional grandiosity, recognizing these traits may not always be obvious to the outside and individual personally.

There are times when losing someone in a relationship or someone you have known passes away, which can be triggers to chemistry imbalance.

Often times if a person is either experiencing traits of mania they will have a lack of sleep or on the other hand if the person may be experiencing signs of depression they may have an increased level of sleep, which are both factors to a possible diagnosis.

You're going to want to watch to see if the eating patterns have changed either more or less, also if the person is consuming more alcohol than normal.

As far as speech patterns the person who made be experiencing and noticeable rapid speech.

On occasion you may also notice if this individual may be speaking about an intimate or deeper spirituality, it is good to have times to have experiences like such, but it affects each and every person differently and can have reverse effects.

For some people they can become socially withdrawn or non-stop babbling.

If you recognize the signs in a loved one or a friend and you are unable to persuade being seen for medical attention and it seems to urgent for a regular appointment, recognizing that the crisis is at the mercy of assistance 911 has been supportive and sheriff task force understand.

• •

Q. **Through this process was there any time that you felt you could hide certain symptoms or secrets?**

A. I always felt and through the interpretation of the mediums of how God worked in Persuasion with me, that I was sent in a secret denial which ultimately put me at risk, it was like I was up against an invisible war with people that supported mental health and medication whether it be my family or those in the health care, a war that they were unsuccessful and I continued mercilessly.

I wouldn't be surprised if other consumers carried a like philosophy.

The risk was, I'm not healthy and I'm not happy so don't mess with me and that justification carried on for years.

Because of these episodes or experiences of wanting to do the right thing and not able to mentally, when I make conscious decisions now with my new chemistry, something people might take for granted, I know the extreme gift of this ability so, in turn I am genuinely more happy and grateful.

Those of you who may be struggling with mental health issues and have these feelings of being unhappy and unhealthy, this is a negative stigma and it actually slows down recovery.

The best thing you can do is take advantage of opportunities to get out whether it's a small walk, coffee or groups where you can learn about Mental Health.

If you are in a situation where you don't feel like you have any friends or family whatever the case may be, I think it's important that, from my own experience I learn to be good company with myself, and sometimes I talk to myself even before sleep and I get really creative, with two different characters that I created and they're always there to help coach me and give encouragements.

Whatever your situation is, try to make the best of it regardless and remember attracting pity's, can be just as strong as attracting HAPPINESSES.

"THERE IS ALWAYS HOPE FOR
UNSETTLED CHEMISTRY"
John Ruonavaara

Conflict In Evaluation

In more clarity what may this person be thinking as this process of evaluation takes its course?

ANSWER

If this person has mixed psychosis and emotions as far as mania, anxiety, and racing thoughts and parts of depression one of the most common feelings is agitation and confusion.

In some ways this individual in this state of mind might conspire the idea that certain groups or family members are working against them.

After experiencing close to 20 if not more emergency room visits related to a mental health crisis with myself, it's miserable you know your failing, you feel lost, your heart tells you things were working, now this empty pain continues to drain inside of you.

Although a greater part of my screenings I was manic, which in some aspects changes the visits experience.

Lots of times in these experiences I would so often while waiting for a mental health professional to screen my visit, whether I should go to the hospital or not and I would rehearse in my head while I wait telling myself I'm doing well and don't need a visit to the hospital.

Because of the hypo mania there were often times Sheriff patrol that were either called to the hospital or part of how I got there.

These experiences were chaos in fact two times running from the hospitals ER, being chased by police on foot.

Failures at this time were so often that they became a reality to my life, I've had many, many, lonely rides in the back of a police car to Marquette General Hospital, 2-hour drive these were dark clouds outside of anything I've ever known.

I was hurting and in ways I felt victimized.

"THE TIDE WAS COMING AND I KNEW IT,
ALTHOUGH I WAS JUST NOT THERE YET"
John Ruonavaara

ER Staff

Looking back now what credit can you give staff working in these crisis units such as the ER?

ANSWER

Both medical team and local police while at the emergency room screening have a tremendous amount of respect and protocol in order to correctly view the crisis.

The individual going through this process so often has a much greater turmoil unseen from the outside and I think crisis workers by having a neutral platform can continue to add to the benefits and have made the experience a lot less stigmatized.

ER Inspiration

Is there any inspiration you might give to someone who may end up in this situation?

ANSWER

First of all, no matter what state or condition the individual is being presented with, I think simply just having confidence that the medical team and procedure is again, simply a medical condition and should be treated as such.

One of the more fitting Inspirations I could think of is that sometimes life is just not fair and to have a safe hold in a way that supports care- taking, in this way you can be Encouraged.

We don't want to forget that this is a temporary health crisis, and your medical team is doing everything in their power to make this as smooth as possible and effective, based on your symptoms.

Tools For Supporters

Are there any words of comfort that you can give to either family or friends that may be visiting the ER at this moment?

ANSWER

Yes, those that are going through the process of getting evaluated oftentimes can be stimulated already and have the stigma of either being manic or depressed or mixed psychosis together.

At this time, it is appropriate for any family or friend, in concept, to try to remain in the back seat while visiting, sometimes just being there with less said and in a way to try to avoid conflict is in our better interest.

The best Comfort one can receive at this time, is to be long-suffering and gentle and to give reminders that support a neutral yet comforting peace.

Anything that "Polarizes the experience" of the person being challenged for example telling them you "love them too often" during the visit or "showing your emotions" too much, and lastly saying things that may put the person in a combat mode, all these things can make the visit harder on the person so basically finding ways to be reserved but yet a neutral support and sometimes it's just with gentle comments.

The reason why I say this is because you're going to want to let the screening person of mental health do their job, that's what they do best, staying out of that process will help decrease stigmatization and preserve relationship.

Illnesses And Their Characters

What are some of the symptoms and interior effects of someone who is diagnosed with a mental illness.

ANSWER

Mania, Depression, Anxiety, three of the main common characters that Define mental disorders.

With Mania you will experience hyper-extended brain chemistry, oftentimes people suffering with mania will use keywords in reference to relate to grandiosity unintentionally, some individuals with extended brain chemistry like this can be very creative, but at the same time very distracted because they are subject and influenced to racing thoughts.

After someone who has had a recovery or is taking medication in order to support a more balanced Life they actually realize because of the effects of mania they we're always jumping to the green grass never making a Content effort with the Here and Now.

With Depression, one may experience a weight of Darkness, physically able to recognize this feeling can be very discouraging.

Normal people have ups and downs and you can recognize and relate although those that have extreme levels of Depression relate its DEPTH and the feeling of how it robs them of every bit of life.

Inside someone who is severely depressed it can affect the same way with the law of attraction for a desired lifestyle.

Although, it works in a way that indirectly is attractive at least to the brain.

Once the haunting feeling begins, and an overwhelming and uncontrollable law of attraction entertains and builds overwhelming amounts of depression into a spiraling downhill.

This is the time they cut off social interactions and even begin to contemplate undesirable grief and discontent.

With Anxiety on the other hand and its crippling effect takes only a twinkling of an eye to activate, it can be likened unto the straw that broke the camel's back.

Some of the worst phobias and powers anxiety has, a person may experience waves of fire going through their body which is very uncomfortable.

If a person is experiencing anxiety one of the best treatments I found was speaking to myself with a very soft tone and slow, coaching the baby to comfort.

Once it recognizes the parent voice it usually and can begin to influence, finding confidence with this procedure continues to strengthen its effect.

As with all other mental health issues anxiety too has a medication that can help decrease its appearances or a drug as needed should you feel the need to take.

Obviously, there are yet so many other challenges in mental health and the diagnosis's including autism, schizophrenia, and seasonal effective disorder, and alike.

Being mindful of other sicknesses collectively helps generalize the scope and possible experience of all the many variables related or unrelated to other possible symptoms in your health.

• •

Q. When would you begin to be concerned in order to identify a symptom that may need to be addressed?

A. It is completely normal to have experiences in part with our human expression, although we want to recognize traits of unhealthy and ongoing trends, while being aware of your concerns it is best to speak with a therapist in order to use first a cognitive approach.

Should your experience not be successful this would be the appropriate time to explain issues with doctor.

Setbacks In Evaluation

So, I'm curious about your 2-hour transport to Marquette on occasion, while seeking medical attention in a hospitalized evaluation, can you explain what that feels like or what's going on in your mind during this process.

ANSWER

Most of the time depending on how bad of a crisis you were getting out of or in the middle of and why you needed to seek medical attention in a hospital, can so often set the stage for transport.

In that regard it can influence the way you feel, for example based on an experience with one of my more manic episodes I was really put into despair personally because I felt totally abandoned from everyone that was supposedly close to me.

This is not strange at all for a person or individual to have these feelings, again these people did not ask for their struggles with mental health and what the challenges and consequences that were deemed of THEMSELVES It's disheartening lonely and cold.

Because of the interior conflict and a sense of exhaustion, while in transport one may actually appeal to the idea of hospitalization.

One of the reasons for an appeal for being hospitalized is that in a way you feel safe and taken care of, and at times the other patients in the unit will tend to entertain or provide some friendship.

QUESTION:

Psychiatric Hospitalization Intro

I would like to get into which I think would be our next phase, what is it like being submitted into a psychiatric treatment Center as a person suffering from mental health crisis?

ANSWER

Well if you have been in this situation before, in a way know what to expect, without discrediting the reality of having to get to this point.

Although if this is your first time being admitted to a psychiatric Treatment Center in order to be put on a medication and monitored, usually the first 24 hours are in a way a little bit stimulating personally because each person being admitted into a unit of such, there is an acclimation period, where are you begin to acclimate to the environment which is the process of feeling comfortable.

If you can kind of imagine already having multiple reasons for being there and then having a bit of an influence with other people that are suffering, it can definitely be disheartening.

In part of the protocol in psychiatric units is that you're able to see or meet with a doctor within the first day in order to immediately start getting things back where you can manage again and the stress load is able to decrease.

I think this is a big part for being encouraged as far as a patient.

Sometimes if the patient is already being prescribed a medication that has a side effect or reaction that is not benefiting their mental status, the Mental Health screener would have put it in the notes that were shipped with you to the unit.

The psychiatric unit normally has the privilege to use drugs to help in a worst-case scenario before you're able to actually see a doctor.

These drugs may be related to crisis related medications not necessarily something you will go home with.

Once you get inside the unit you can eventually get to a point where you can feel home with yourself as awkward as it might have seemed.

Often times when getting into the unit they would help me out with either some yogurt or sandwiches, it is common for them to ask if you would be interested, because so often those in the crisis exhaust many hours without having to eat anything and also draining their emotional and psychological status.

The nature and how you are received by these nurses and team care for the unit is reassuring, they understand the medical situation and are not trying to give you the impression you're being penalized.

Upon being admitted they're going to want to check Vital Signs and ask questions related to your Mental Health crisis and also General Health.

For the safety of that unit they will go through most of your clothes and make sure that you are in a safe place with others and may ask you to place certain items in their locker in order to make this experience limited from any other hazards.

....

Q. Is there any reason why it may be difficult to acclimate under these circumstances?

A. Well to design a concept and support for this question as far as being acclimated, its much like riding on an airplane and you begin to feel turbulence and the stigma of your experience begins to escalate.

On occasion depending on how others may be responding or acting in the hospitals ward may impact how you may respond.

Wards Exprience

What did you observe about others that were in a like experience in these psychiatric units?

ANSWER

I guess I've noticed times when there were not so many people admitted into the hospital and I guess in a way it's not as entertaining as when there are more people in the unit.

Even though there may be people also at their worst, there was a sense of friendship and family amongst us at least for the greater part of those seeking treatment and its evaluation.

I could not help but to look and see others that have pain as well and I guess in a way it was a comfort to know that I was not alone, often times struggling outside of the unit it's easy to conspire this lonesomeness in life.

On one occasion it was a Sunday evening and news amongst us was being spread of a very big guy being admitted into the unit, and I think immediately people started picking up this unstable vibe and he was definitely a big guy, after seeing him I myself began to be concerned.

Often times when this type of experience especially someone who is being admitted it's like getting into the unit all over again and being acclimated to that person's chemistry.

I remember thinking to myself that I better walk past him just to dismiss the idea that he's not going to attack me.

He was in rough shape and suffering most likely from schizophrenia and in this case, most likely he was without his medicine for a while and was really bad off.

I remember going past him and he was mumbling and talking to himself and talking seem to be struggling with hallucinations.

We all kind of got used to the environment and they must have got him on medication immediately after being admitted because a day or so passes and I saw him in the cafeteria early morning having coffee and watching basketball on the TV and more relaxed.

So, I was just getting up in the morning and I walked into the cafeteria and I remember thinking to myself I hope he's doing better.

I was always capable of having a very natural calm and most of any experience in the psych ward I think even if I'm nervous or upset I would have success in keeping my composure.

So, I began to fill my cup of coffee and usually they have regular coffee in the morning so it helps people wake up that was a great part for the mornings.

Well I said good morning to him and he responded back and asked what my shirt said, it was an Aeropostale shirt, I returned the answer and he said he liked my shirt and I thanked him and distracted the question with the basketball he was watching on TV.

He kind of just nodded his head and said it was on when he came in.

It's just so amazing seeing people at their very worst and then being able to have normal conversations after a day of being medicated he was calm and such a really nice guy.

I think just keeping in mind that these people and myself we did not ask for the situations of these medical conditions, so when you see medicine and through the aid of a Medical teams' assistance make a difference in someone's life it's a victory.

. . . .

Q. **You talked about this composure, what do you think your instinct was while be admitted?**

A. At that time I knew it was not for me to decide the outcome of another person's struggles, I did not want to get involved and I did not want to feel involved, but rather more of an observation.

Although, when the opportunity presented itself and the occasion was fitting, I willingly tried to give encouragement. There was definitely a composed, soothed, hesitance, in the stigma of my instinct, as an auto defense for my individualism and space for recovery.

QUESTION:

Strengths While Suffering

During the prolonged duration of your mental health status and before you were able to get successful with a diagnosis and medication what were some of your strengths?

ANSWER

I think it's important to take this time to recognize one of my greatest supports in the life of my illness and Beyond and this was my mother, she was a true symbol of self-sacrificing love.

She also was an extra-ordinary neutral and was not at all in position to take sides although very patient always soft spoken.

She only saw what was in my heart she also understood that I was suffering and had a very difficult time making choices.

A notable strength within myself was the ability to be visionary in perception.

I would open up to just about anyone who would give me the time of day to listen to me and talk about ideas and evolving concepts.

I had a custom of doing day in day out and I really got good at discussing the idea and reading facial expressions to see if they were following me.

It seemed to me that these were building blocks as far as understanding terminology in the course of explaining something.

I feel using cognition has a biological effect on chemistry in a way that was actually much like physical exercises enhancing my mechanical brain energized through creativity.

One of my friends kept saying to me, all talk no action.

I took him up on that offer alone on the jest of what I just explained as far as how the biologics often times can increase in strength and it's almost in a sense of a physical construct that increases one's cognition.

With potential order to build masterpieces in communication in order to continue to enhance, build, and observe transparencies.

It seems because part of my mind was wounded, I would try all the harder to succeed my vision on things and ideas I guess that was my sense of entertainment in a way.

These characters as far as inventive thinking, would in a way influence or stimulate my chemistry in a way to hold a grandiose State of Mind but I guess maybe in a little bit more technical statue.

It wasn't just one or two subjects it was every possible subject and product on the market whether it was a software platforms or mechanical property to material and functionality.

I do not know what the extent Curious George was but I think I got him beat! I guess to summarize my strength, even if I was wounded mentally I was Relentless and Visionary and I think that's a defining character of being strong through this process.

In fact, one of my experiences I was talking to this person that came in contact with and I thought he would be a good person to explain my idea or fabrication on one of my projects.

I literally got halfway into explaining it and I did not see this one coming but he totally got up from his chair and left.

I think it's kind of funny now because the monstrosity of its way in the process of explaining must have completely overwhelmed his thought on this matter.

I guess I've had multiple similar occasions like this in my life.

Sometimes it was so simple and that's when I would get a little bit frustrated because most of the time I would be shut down or walked away from, was from stubbornness and personal interest only.

Even though my illness had its influences, I was still naturally inclined into a technical world.

....

Q. Did you while having these spurs of inventions take any big risks as far maxing out credit cards or careless spending?

A. Yes in some ways, although for some reason I was reluctant not to exceed high depth, I personally felt if my idea is granted and meant I should not need a loan, and I kind of stuck to that concept on all my ideas.

QUESTION:

Draining Mania

In counter reaction to someone who may be experiencing medication in response to symptoms of mania, can you identify what that feeling might be like?

ANSWER

Someone who is experience high levels of mania become very irrational.

I guess from the outside you may observe sporadic body movements and rapid speech alongside of these symptoms.

There also is the inability to effectively communicate with this individual.

When someone is struggling with high levels of mania there is a natural tendency for that individual to make assumptions on simple things that you may relate to or talk about.

Because Mania creates an inferior self-protection of the ego, it is not uncommon at all for this person to be overprotective or on guard.

Common traits to someone who is challenged in this way has a strong inferior complex and noticeable insecurities.

So, I guess to get into answering the question about how medication responds and what that person may be questioning about is the reality of suppressed chemistry.

Which is the very intent for medication and its intervention.

Sometimes the first part of being medicated underneath these standards can oftentimes give the impression that their life and everything they enjoy has been taken away.

This reality can bring a despair personally because it definitely dampens the enthusiasm.

It's almost like in reference to going on a diet you never signed up for.

So now at this point you may begin to cultivate a sense of conflict against medication your medical team and doctor.

I guess you can kind of imagine why it is necessary for some recovering patients with illnesses of such to be placed on a court order.

In some cases, the thought of running away or quitting the medication is a conspiracy that consumes the individuals every thought.

Treating illnesses with medication and with some individual caseworkers and therapist are the most humane way to deal with these inconveniences of imbalanced chemistry.

The advice I would give to someone who may be in this status, if it begins to become a false reality and a false report that actually turns your attention away from this medication intervention, it is very beneficial to have a counselor that you can open up and look at models that are working and try to improve and polish that model and work on smaller things that may be related to helping the cause in the same effort.

Increased levels of cognition and communicating effectively can enhance and help overlook things that may be otherwise seem very difficult.

• •

Q. **What do you think is one of the biggest obstacles regarding medical intervention under these circumstances?**

A. It is very difficult to remove the clouds of doubt and it's even harder when these patterns are part of your daily life. My only encouragement is start building a list of things to be grateful for and take passion in daily reflections on these simplicities and begin those small and new levels of appreciation, eventually new healthy patterns become obvious.

QUESTION:

Communication Tactics

The many challenges of effective communication can be a struggle, can you provide some tips or ideas that may help?

ANSWER

If you are talking with someone who has mental health challenges it is important to stay on key as far as being consistent with tone and simplicity.

Another important characteristic is to allow time between questions without getting frustrated or giving the sense that you may be.

Someone who may be experiencing an irritated manic state may make it difficult and even seem impossible to communicate with.

Sometimes the best thing to do under these circumstances is to do nothing at all, their levels of frustration is not on account of your personal relationship but, rather more of an interior conflict.

If you have suggestions and you want to try to help it is best to wait for the moment where they seem more relaxed this way we can find simple suggestions that may work.

Someone who is severely depressed, just by saying kind compliments and being sincere as a host in order to cater may perk them up as much as a cup of coffee.

Moments like this where you show compassion and gentle kindness can often lift their spirits, although this kindness and compassion and less talk can also have an impact on those that are extremely frustrated.

If you have creative ideas and ways to make a difference and be nice, it can actually make the experience that much more effective and enjoyable, I think we all enjoy seeing people happy.

The tactic of not getting wrapped up in their stigma and showing your gentle side and help can build a stronger trust relationship.

It is important to have times where you can both sit down and feel comfortable talking about little things that may help, but for the greater part, just being there.

There are many ways to communicate without talking, as long-suffering as it might seem, there are benefits.

I want to acknowledge the benefits of going on a car ride and why it's a great opportunity for talking and soothing its remedy as therapeutic, often times when struggling we don't always feel comfortable being directly looked at, so with soft music and exploring our drive can help take our mind off our struggles and feel more adapt to talking.

Car rides create an indirect atmosphere and relieves the pressure of one-on-one.

· ·

Q. **Could attending certain support groups in your community have an effect on better communication?**

A. Yes, sometimes curtain mental health clinics hold group meetings that are open to consumers receiving care, most communities are aware of the National Alliance on Mental Illness (NAMI) which is a nationwide grassroots advocacy group, representing people affected by mental illness. Designed to open assertion with expressing and dealing with mental health issues with group meetings, oftentimes orchestrated by mental health consumers themselves.

Team Care With Doctor

As far as one and one with your doctor and staff how would you explain the most effective way to address Med changes and or side effects?

ANSWER

As a patient and receiving Medical Care from a doctor it is important to have an open dialogue.

Before the doctor will prescribe medication, they are going to ask questions related to what you may be experiencing, in return the doctor is going to try to find a medication with the least amount of side effects.

Sometimes depending on the extremity of symptoms, you may be experiencing, a certain drug would be prescribed that often times have temporary side effects.

I think we need to bear in mind that in some cases the benefits of the medication outweigh the consequences of the side effects in order to establish a more balanced chemistry with the individual.

I think it's easy and natural for someone who is challenged with mental health issues to establish the idea of an immediate results.

When I talk about an open dialogue I think it's good to share ideas and thoughts on where you would like to be, in a way that can be accepting for both your medical team and yourself.

If you do decide to look up and learn about the illness on-line and even look up medications, I think it's important to be educational about it but, also an open-minded approach for the very reason that medications affect people differently and we all have different biological makeups.

It is important if you do favor a certain procedure or medication that may alternate the benefits in a way that supports compatibility, you're going to want to address the possibility with your doctor.

Although, during your recovery you may be on a medication and it might be the exact drug you are looking for, but the regiment as far as portion maybe the only factor.

So, in some cases your doctor is going to want to exhaust every possibility of having an effective medication before getting fixed again all over on a new one remembering the process can be prolonged.

You and your doctor are a team and by learning to express details and ask questions about yourself can help the experience and understanding.

I think we need to keep in mind that not all doctor visits can be enjoyable especially if we're struggling somewhere in my life and it just does not seem like it's coming together.

There were times in my recovery when I was incompetent and not able to be a full contributing factor in the decisions that had to be made in order to preserve Health once again.

I remember going to doctor visits feeling so incomplete and frustrated these are the emotions that sometimes are part of our life's experience in recoveries process.

For those of you whether you are family or friends and support for an individual that may be suffering it is important to keep in mind this is not an easy task for these situations to be in, reserved reactions and communicating are your greatest strength.

....

Q. Is there any kind of prep work that may help before appointments?

A. I think bringing along positive acknowledgments about yourself, and questions you feel fitting for this moment. In some ways trying not to set expectations too high.

Community Tools

What are some tools that can help a community as an effort to recognize those with mental health challenges?

ANSWER

City, State, or Federal level, I think would be beneficial to have exercise facilities in order to help individuals gain self-worth and value of the health benefits of being in shape.

Basically, a way to increase chances for successful employment, being part of an incentive program, I think definitely
increases the value.

I would like to see small housing cubicles that while in transition they're able to take the burden off finding an apartment and focus on the elementary phases of recovery.

It is dark enough for an individual to close down inside because of this challenge, I think without having an alternative way to increase that person's chance to have a better and sustaining life, it's consequently derailing.

People with mental health issues tend to be left behind I see some of it in my own town, I think communities need a hub in order to show support and compassion as far as a way to interact and open to the community.

We have the technology to build a software program designed as a docking port in order to build personal profiles for the individual and increase chances of recovery whether it's through an exercise program or social interactions or a sustained level of mood, it's very difficult for one struggling to collect this information and use it wisely in order to support sustainability and increase their chances into a bigger insight.

Basically, creating a scoreboard simulation that gives profiling details and validation in accordance for documented reflections.

• •

Q. Do you think with the correct motive and support, it is possible to reverse the stigma of what mental illnesses are capable of?

A. On a normal day for someone who is not suffering with any significant mental health issues or diagnosis, we can find more recognizable patterns of achievements, although on the other side of the spectrum, those that meet the struggles of mental health, achievements can be a foreign attribute.

I think creating the potential for hope with tools of convenient creativity and possible valued software programs that show even the smallest increments of improvements in reference to collecting data and proving confidence of self-worth and instituting the power to rise above.

I truly believe we need to start showing greater light at the tunnels end.

Work-Related Difficulties

Did you have any experiences that may have made it difficult for you to hold a job and if so, how does that relate to others who might have a like experience?

ANSWER

I could not work or concentrate for the life of me. I had every intention to work and be constructive on a job site, but through the reality of my illness I was failing.

I remember telling my working partners that I was feeling good today and shouldn't have a problem, because of this struggle it begins to become a growing concern, it's very frustrating going through the emotions and trying to stay focused and end up being distracted over little things.

It wasn't long into the day and I would just get so overwhelmed, I would be thinking about other parts of my life and could not just drop the thought and move on, and naturally I would become obsessed, whether it was a project I was working on or the frustrations of life in general.

I was always so amazed how people could go to work every day and be able to concentrate enough to continue working it just blew my mind, I didn't know any other alternative because my chemistry was always kind cockeyed or in that matter unbalanced.

I want to clarify that in my diagnosis for bipolar there was a part that was not being accounted for.

My second diagnosis of bipolar schizoid-affective disorder, the reason why I bring this up is because close to 15 years I was unable to concentrate on work because of my chemistry that was not being medicated for, only to be found later with the extended evaluation.

For 15 years I continue to have hyper-extended brain chemistry which made it impossible for any type of concentration or determination and follow through with every job I encountered.

Working on a job whether you have states of mania or depression consequently responds the same way.

I don't want to leave the impression that working is out of the question and discourage, those that are honestly up and doing what they can for what's available I want to encourage.

I also want to encourage those who may be encountered with the challenges of mental and work-related success.

I feel it is very important to be active in the community as part of a due diligence even as a volunteer and being active can also play part to a social life to new opportunities you would not have otherwise sitting at home.

•••

Q. Can you explain the frustration of mood related to overwhelming job failures?

A. I guess every attempt of my work experience had a conditional mindset as if the type of work I was working on eventually became a validation of mood.

Basically, it felt like what I was working on projected itself a mood mostly very undesirable.

These overwhelming experiences literally drained any competence of composed healthy work ethic daily.

This mood and struggle went on for years, many years.

The only thing that kept me going was my sustaining spirit, determination and the curiosity that things might get better.

Non-Medicated

We understand by experience that a lot of people intentionally go off their medication, is there any time of your life that you may have gone through with something like this and maybe bring us an idea of what that experience was like?

ANSWER

I have one experience that really stands out other than times where I may have missed one or two doses.

Most of my medicated experience I was diligent in the faithfulness of taking medication, although there were times where I wanted to go without the medication and display a sense of independence from any type of psychiatric medication.

The fabrication of these ideas of entertaining life without medication begin with being frustrated with unsuccessful and loss hope in recovery.

I only contemplated the idea of no meds because there was not an opportunity for me to successfully act on it.

In the middle of November of 2012, the convenience of having a friend making arrangements to move to North Dakota in the Williston location and begin working as part of a Service Company in the Bakken was attractive to me.

It was an opportunity to escape and display my first time the ability to use my chemistry in Independence outside of medication.

I packed my bags and left my hometown and have to say through this experience I held my ground for a while.

Shortly after the third month I was there I started seeing increasing levels of concern, but because of the manic hype I was able to overlook the consequences that yet continued to eventually become unavoidable.

Even while I was having my successes working in the oil field and taking tests and passing them in order to ensure safety, I had a contact still in place with my Mental Health Team back home.

I was also hung up on the idea of sending lengthy text to family and friends in which elevated the concern because of its grave grandiosity and difficulty to understand.

I was comfortable for a while with this position of no medication in my system but then I personally started feeling the effects.

Heightened hype was enjoyable but, it only lasts so long and without having the ability to concentrate in the way that supports stability and make choices that benefit a balanced life, it is inevitable that it eventually begins to strike.

That's when I started making phone calls and having more emotional breakdowns and worries and I think what's important about a situation like this is you can lose trust with yourself really fast, which then begins to take a toll on every bit of your successes.

I think anyone that understands what it feels like to be in a crisis I would say when you are off your medication for a longer period of time and you go into a crisis it's that much more magnified.

Alcohol was never really part of my life, on February 14th 2013 that evening me and my friend partied, my first and only time being drunk.

I felt very connected to the world around me and within me as one, probably one of my biggest epiphanies or Awakening while in a way my chemistry was being jolted or definitely overworked the very next day, I remember hearing in the news about an asteroid lighting the skies in Russia and making an impact, and because of how my brain was wired it was significant to me.

I was hyper-extended with my chemistry more than I've ever experienced in my life, but it happened to come at a time of instability.

The content of this epiphany was a mixture between my spiritual interpretations and the greater philosophy of being introduced to how people feel a deeper connection under the influence of alcohol. I remember as I would work with my co-partners, my mind could not stay concentrated very well I would shutter with tears and then quickly wiping away and try to avoid showing to those around me.

I was a really talkative person sometimes but had a very difficult time compartmentalizing my life in a way that can show balance and valued decisions.

I think my experiences demonstrate extremities of the human spirit, although the harmony of that can be difficult, especially without correct brain chemistry.

This experience was chaotic and much like an unquenchable fire, emotionally and psychologically, would not advise anyone on these terms who have reoccurring mental health symptoms and currently receiving medical mental health care.

••

Q. How can you help those to keep their focus on recovery?

A. I don't think we want to suppress or take away our intuition to dream and look ahead, in fact I think part of our recovery is dependent on these characters.

The focus comes when we build together with dreams and daily recovery.

I can't emphasis enough how important of be more consciously aware and grateful on even small appreciations.

To help focus more, is also being prideful of ourselves and what we care for around us each and every day.

Relationship

Can you express any relationships that you may have had during this time in your recovery, and the impact it may have had on you and your time together?

ANSWER

Through my church community at the time I was attracted a girl named Elizabeth we met and got to know each other only a short time and we were in a position to make a decision on staying together, so I we scheduled a marriage for the 8th of January of 2000.

Around this time and about 5 years into our marriage my chemistry was somewhat more stable.

We spent around 10 years together having 4 boys and 1 girl, beautiful children and smart.

It's understandable that not every day is a wedding day and it only got more obvious after about 5 years into the marriage.

Things started to fall apart, I was obsessively assuming a lot of stuff that was not even happening, like creating ideas and attracting the perversion that she was having an affair and this accumulated a mistrust in the integrity for our relationship.

I began to take more and more risks, as these risks increased I would make an account to justify my risks by developing more false accusations.

Through these accusations and risks, decay began to be more obvious, I have become a different person and was not at all desirable to be around.

I can imagine now how very difficult it would have been for Elizabeth to love someone and find traits that were not at all apparent on the day of proposal.

Honestly, I in complete confidence believe my judgment was altered by sickness although the disguise was nearly impossible to truly identify.

I'm speaking first hand, with direct experience in the very power of justification under the perversion of twisted chemistry.

I slowly became a mechanical manipulator, I consciously began to back my assumptions to take more risks.

This is the very intent of what goes on in a person's brain when they are trying to create malicious attacks conspired by empty conclusions.

Even if they were empty conclusions I still created a desire awkwardly to believe in them, so naturally I was hurt but also very confused and distracted by this false illusion.

To understand hyper-extended brain chemistry, in example with this window space and the tip to the magnitude on how muddy the waters can actually get.

It eventually got to the point where these malicious attacks, lost all confidence and the dignity of being respected and most of all loved.

I truly have to give credit, as far as Elizabeth she got to know me and that's who she married, unfortunately the storm God was allowing at this time needed new terms in order to restore.

I remember her telling me that you used to have so many friends and you were always just so nice to all these people and now I don't know you at all.

The mercy of our separation was imminent, the chaotic experience of that chemistry even with the best intentions, I still failed miserably.

We all go through bumps in the road but this was a multi psychological plot based on the ability to manipulate and justify what I assumed and a variety of strange obsessions I entertained through illness related falsehoods and its influence of poor judgment.

Strange obsessions and psychological twisting had a strange and dark attraction.

And because of hyper-extended brain chemistry it continued to spiral around in my head, this is what made it nearly impossible to stop and the very reason for separation.

Because of the incompetence of my mental status after a short time of being separated in our marriage I become frustrated and even more careless which consequently end up having an affair.

The deck of cards of that relationship was finally ended in a divorce, relationships are not a game although I prolonged the theory that it could be, it's astounding and sad that mental illness can become such an uncontrolled deceiving pollution.

Your heart says one thing and your mind continues to be the dictating force.

I was not aware that my mind was actually doing this until I was able to get medication to benefit normal chemistry.

Honestly at the time I remember looking around I remember so much in so much detail and having all the right intentions in a sense, but still influenced by twisted versions in chemistry.

Because of what was going on in my head and it was not directly related to the core I remember almost dumbfounded on her final decision to leave.

I believe now this experience was not my own and that God seen fit that this season would come.

It definitely gave me some depth to what it feels like to have strange obsessions dictate the outcome of your life and how they are influenced and so often times can be overlooked.

I tried using spiritual platforms in my church community to outsmart its chemical twist, but its magnitude was much bigger than I expected.

The words and obvious characters of insight I'm using to describe this experience had no reference or order during this period of suffering, I would not understand this if my chemistry didn't receive its recovery.

· ·

Q. **Do you think because of the depth of this madness you are better able to understand those who may carry like patterns?**

A. I would say it definitely opens the possibly.

QUESTION:

Suicide

During this prolong recovery have you had any moments where you were a harm to yourself or others or have any attempted suicide?

ANSWER

Yes, on two of more significant occasions, directly after the reality of having to have a divorce set in.

The other was when I was at my worst in the hospital after increased levels of hallucinations and voices.

The first attempt, at one point I just decided this pain, darkness and lonesomeness are just not worth it and I kept reflecting on all the stuff that I have lost it was disheartening.

I knew at times what the good side of me wanted to do but was unable to deliver and in that matter, I felt like such a failure.

I put nicotine patches all over my body to try to give myself a cardiac arrest.

So, I remember late that evening and opening all these bags of nicotine patches and placing them all over my chest stomach area legs and arms.

I wanted to distract myself while the patches hopefully worked, so I decided to go for a ride out in the country away from the idea of being recognized in public.

I remember about 6 miles away from town opening my window and throwing my telephone out so there would be no way of contacting me or finding my location.

I continued to drive eventually I got to smaller town on the outskirts of our city, stopped in my vehicle on a side road near the highway and opened my door and throwing up all over on the side of the road.

I was beginning to get very dizzy and felt very sick, from the effects of overdosing on nicotine.

I had a half a gallon of grape juice in my vehicle at the time and I remember after barfing slugging it down to hopefully decrease the amount of nicotine's effect in my blood.

I didn't have much time to wait things out because as I was sitting in my car it was not long that a sheriff patrol car seen my lights on his normal Patrol route.

I did not know if my family called the police because I sent a text to my mom that evening stressing my overwhelming despairs.

So as the car approached me I found out that it was actually the sheriff patrol car and that's when I began an accelerating high-speed chase.

The chase lasted about a little over a half an hour or so and was able to be settled peacefully by multiple officers that evening.

After explaining to the officers about what was going on they were able to transport me to Portage Health in Hancock.

I have become a regular concern in the community for so many numbers of years, especially having to be hospitalized 13 times in this process.

So, I guess the officers had the idea that I was going through another one of my episodes.

Later after I'm going to health screening at the hospital I was transported to Marquette General for an evaluation.

I want to encourage anyone who is reading this information that I am with the intent to educate about the life and experience and struggles to someone who is going through a mental health crisis.

This information is not provided to give the wrong influence or impression, but rather, support the idea of why we need each other and recognition to medical staff and our supports.

Probably one of the most difficult times in my illness and the history of what I've been through was when I began to have hallucinations and voices with anxiety and confusion.

I knew I was not stable enough to be by myself, so I asked my staff to help me get into a group home in the community somewhere.

They succeeded with getting me a place for mental health people to live and feel safe.

I thought these hallucinations would go away although I was wrong and eventually it got to the point where they needed to get me to the hospital.

I was still very unsettled while in the hospital with attempts of self- harm, shortly after they were able to use a medication to help with this suffering.

I received medication to continue and was able to have a successful discharge.

I did eventually end up facing fines and the suspended license for a period of time in result of this crisis.

I want to encourage anyone who has had experience like this or is currently going through a recovery with mental health, that if you begin to recognize symptoms we need to be free to reach out or seek medical attention.

QUESTION:

Watching Angels

In your own experience how did you view other people that were diagnosed with a mental disorder whether it would be in the hospital or in your community?

ANSWER

I think we all share a common stigma, that feeling of not being understood and I guess in a way that the world has turned against us.

I remember Early Mornings in the hospital we would come together and have a goals group to start the day.

The staff would ask what is it that you would like as a goal for today.

So many mornings I remember patience's coming together in this Lakeview Lounge.

I remember distinctly each patient answering the question, you could see the struggle in their faces and their body movement of not being comfortable.

In a way because of their struggles, challenges and reasons for being hospitalized, the nature of their body movements was similar to a puppy that was abused by his master.

These crippling effects shown consistent throughout all the times I was hospitalized.

It's like the baby inside them was sick and was not able to be understood and consequently having to be in this unfortunate condition.

I would say about 50% if not more on some days had to struggle with coming up with a goal.

None-the-less the hospital staff was clearly identified to treat them with a medical condition rather than a personality or disadvantage, and this was obvious I think they have a very neutral yet strong front in order to keep the respect of the individual separated from their weaknesses.

It was not uncommon to spend a lot of different times and kind of the lodge area of the unit where other members could also sit down.

Our communication wasn't always active sometimes I remember sitting there amongst maybe three or four other patients and having just small talk and then moments of silence, so often this was just the reality of our conditions.

Even if there were moments of silence, I still observe so much, oftentimes if there was someone who was upset and was walking the halls and would make comments out loud whether they were directed to the staff or just anyone that might hear.

I paid attention to how other people would react in order to in a way analyze how they felt in situations that could be negative stigma for their experience at the moment.

Usually if they would make a face of concern and turn their face away with sudden body movements usually with their legs to readjust, I could tell they were sensitive to any kind of negative drama.

The workload of each individual while being treated and evaluated in these psychiatric hospitals, may differ from time to time but we've been there and we know the feelings.

To be honest we had a common goal that was not discussed much but we all wanted to have peace with one another so even if there are one or two people that may be upset at the time we always had a desire that that individual could get help and usually their able to become part of that peace token that was unsaid but felt.

For the majority amount of the patience seeking treatment we were usually good company to each other and they were as an indirect family with common acceptances.

On the other hand, in my community because I was seeking mental health treatment with an intensive treatment team which was a branch of the regular outpatient, I come more in contact with others that I would see periodically through the weeks.

This gave me an opportunity to learn how to build trust and friendship without pressing requirements of friendship back.

Often times I would simply say good morning and usually the tone of the voice I would respond carefully and soft.

Sometimes I would be visiting with an older lady at my apartment complex that has been in state Institution hospitals in her past and I always enjoyed being next to her while I smoked my cigarettes.

Sometimes in the mid-afternoon she would be smoking out on the bench and I would sit down next to her and I would not say anything for a couple minutes and maybe just a simple hello upon seeing her was enough.

In return if I got a hello back from her that was a victory for me.

Slowly over time I've gained her trust I built friendships, I seen the elementary phases and sometimes building a no-pressure environment, whether you are diagnosed with a mental disorder or not we all have a story in life and we all want to be liked and acknowledged.

The Compassion that builds over me is instilled by the pain that I've been through and the life I've endured.

Most of the time when I do extend my help and support, it is with the quest for nothing in return, it means more to me to show compassion.

I listen to the prompting and I am consciously aware of no precondition ideas or circumstances that would undermine or interfere with obvious prompts to contribute, outside of any sect, religion, personalities or lifestyles.

It's easy to generalize particular concepts that help devalue our choices and find secret willingness to justify in order to have the free card and ignorance not to help.

A certain level of honesty is definitely involved, whether it is someone with mental health issues or our struggling neighbors.

Therapist

What are some building blocks or tools that are beneficial to talk about with a therapist and what are some of the best ways to address issues?

ANSWER

I think for the first couple times seeing your therapist it is good to get to explore what was working for you in the past and what you would like to try to achieve now.

This may take a couple visits before you realize what stage you can begin at as far as the challenges you are facing and how to find elementary stages to begin building your goals.

There is also a therapeutic side which is equally important as setting goals.

Most of my experiences with therapist is they are there to listen and cater to what interest you can benefit from in this visit.

If you are intending to try to achieve goals and talk about ways on how you can begin to see results, I would advise finding very simple things that you can do without putting the bar too high.

It is not uncommon at all to have a desire to make bigger strides and want to accomplish more but we want to be encouraged on the small stuff, that we are able to do and talk about how we were successful in doing these elementary type goals.

Medical Breakthrough

How long was this prolonged recovery and diagnosis of bipolar continue, before you're able to actually have a breakthrough?

ANSWER

I was diagnosed in high school of the Year 1997 and continued with that diagnosis until 2014, a 17-year struggle with trying to find medication and handling everyday stresses and 13 hospital visits to a psychiatric evaluation center, or more commonly known as psych ward.

Prior to moving back from North Dakota and receiving medication and a treatment plan I was on the drug Fortuna or at least about a year's time.

This medication seems to help pretty good at first but then became very uncomfortable and had the feeling like my skin was crawling.

On April 1st of 2014 I was admitted into the hospital which was probably my most memorable crisis.

My mental status at that time was suicidal and it was shown while I was in the hospital, which marked the time I cut my wrist.

After getting out of the hospital on the 10th of April I had multiple visits with my psychiatrist and I was getting injections for medication alongside of some pills.

The turning point in my medical health condition with the diagnosis of bipolar was for the first time being considered bipolar schizoid-affective disorder.

Which would include a mood disorder manic depressive and also traits of schizophrenia that have a similar effect but not as dominant.

This medical breakthrough and observation from my medical team and doctor, was formally off the radar, what some people may consider voices in their head, my chemistry was under an influence indirectly and it affected in a like manner.

So instead of hearing voices it was actually my philosophies influencing and polluting bad chemistry with having hyper-extended chemistry as I mentioned before.

On May 1st 2014 I was introduced to the drug clozapine.

While with a visit with my doctor we talked about this new diagnosis and the effects it can have.

Prior to all the medications I have taken in the past, clozapine was the drug for the first time I was able to look in the mirror and shake hands with who I saw.

Because of the drugs side effects, I was advised by my doctor decided that I would stay in a mental health group home.

It was a good choice because I had the episode that I cannot remember much of until I end up 2 hours away in Marquette at the psychiatric hospital.

After some small adjustments I was able to return to the group home.

It was very intriguing to me I remember going outside at the group home and having a smoke it was a sunny evening, I've never felt this much at peace.

I've had so many times in my past where I would be sitting in my truck outside of the location I was going to visit and just thinking to myself if I could only stop my mind from going so fast this was not uncommon for me to think this at all.

I remember just standing there smoking my cigarette no one else was outside at the time, in concept it was like riding a hurricane for so many years and suddenly wake up in the dream of riding the eye.

As the days went by on this medication and I was able to return to my apartment, for the first time I knew the clock was not an issue anymore.

If you think about it how about being in a situation where you know what the right choice to make something work or have a successful relationship with someone, but so unable to deliver.

A polluted mind, but a good heart, sick and helpless.

With the influence and the effects of my illness it was nearly impossible to see through to clarity, everyone was looking for, including me.

And to keep in mind, this breakthrough was not no instant gratification, while the head was wounded mentally the infrastructure and psychological philosophies influencing every motive, needed to be on my own part reevaluated and sometimes huge files over time slowly became decompressed and reorganized.

Definitely processing information much better.

QUESTION:

Recovery Benefits

Can you identify what you are able to do now more effectively or have seen an increase as far as improvement on your life with this medication?

ANSWER

At every level I was failing at in the past it is becoming more and more obvious as I continue to draw the health security of what I'm able to do on medication, that is treating the issue that was ignored for so long.

After riding the hurricane for so long this medication with clozapine as a last resort medication and lithium the brain became empty and the only things that shown were the things that were important for the most part and by choice what I wanted to focus on, more less natural chemistry.

I guess a better way to explain it was instead of having unrelated multiple choices influenced by distorted patterns I was Consciously now able to make valued decisions.

There were side effects with the medication when I first started but after a half a year passed, I start seeing less and less side effects and they slowly diminished.

In my old chemistry I would go to certain family events or places around town and even before entering into the group of people I would have already have a preconceived assumed in theory that conflict was at large, almost like having a chip on my shoulder every time.

It is miraculous for me to show up to a place to visit and have absolutely nothing on my mind and so well accepting of the moment.

It was like using an ineffective GPS in the fog and getting frustrated, then to having multi-dimensional and effective GPS navigating your way through the evening and perfecting the experience.

New chemistry gave me the ability to relaxed and totally become myself in how I would have always wanted to be.

It's really neat even now with my new chemistry I can seem withdrawn and quiet and then I have these spontaneous sparks of life whether I am humorous about something or contributing to a conversation or just being the child in myself and laughing and having a good time.

It is very remarkable to have the feelings I do on this new medication I really and truly feel like a human being now, never really had normal ups and downs like everyone else never really able to hold a job and do good work with concentration enough to benefit, never able to really have good relationships as far as friendships around the community and also at a social media platform.

It catches me by surprise when people are nice to me I guess I feel so unworthy of anyone's friendship just because my mind is not used to people liking me.

I would have to say at this time one of the biggest and most significant benefits of having effective medication is that it supports a human natural and the ability to go through my day without an extended ego continually influencing grandiosity.

I think now my ego is normal and my happiness is natural and genuine.

QUESTION

As far as mental health at a national level what would you foresee as far as improvements and procedures that could cater to the interest of mental health patients and the extended study of Mental Health-care?

ANSWER

Without a doubt we have come long ways with the intervention of medicine, and that is not about to change.

It is one of the most Humane ways to work with people that have mental health conditions.

Outside of being medicated I think we need to look for more ways to give an analysis, through the use of coordinating smart software analyzing equipment for exercising devices.

These exercises would be in conjunction to how the creative brain makes its response and in part with gracefulness.

Allowing the consumer to exercise mediums that would initially grade performance of that person's ability to function at that level.

There would also be coordinating equipment that would evaluate the consumer's ability to exercise efficiency with the mechanical brain in reference to increasing the person's motor skills.

Part of this grading process for the consumer in a way to support a scoreboard, is to go through the process and understand the balance between the two both, mechanical brain and creative brain.

For example, if the machine is requiring effective motor skills in order to be effective with coordinating certain touch buttons when they were lit up, the grading process would give a balance to how fast and how slow and then beginning to find a balance between the two polarities.

There would also be endurance grading adaptive in order to give people an incentive to increased levels of endurance during exercise.

We need to look at the evaluation daily and then begin to see charts that can show our progression.

A lot of our consumers that are suffering with mental health issues and are currently taking medication for these symptoms in order to sustain a level of life that can be supported, often times turn into sitting ducks, I know first-hand and its suppressive consequences.

Just going to the gym for these consumers is not good enough they need to have a grading process and an evaluation they can look at and see improvements and as team support, find ways to give courage.

The idea behind exercising motor skills and being able to have an expanded evaluation from time to time and see where they're doing well and give statistical encouragement as long side with coaching.

Many times, people with strong mechanical brains often times lose sight of how to use the creative brain.

As far as new theories that may develop overtime also with the electronic age we also may be able to use frequencies in order to help certain parts of the brain tissue related to that experience, by building stronger tolerances or ability to callus harmful thought process and possible intervention to avoid hallucinations.

The building components in order to achieve stronger sense of self- worth and respect, pivots a lot depending on posture, clothing design, and well-groomed.

I have looked into the concept of a unisex clothing design that has the ability to give the impression of being comfortable and still having a high expectation, for the individuals.

Those that have the desire to achieve Higher Goals and meet the expectations of this recovery program I believe they should be honored and have the option to pick apartment supplies or self-care from the gift shop to new supplies or items that are related to their goals being met.

As the housing facility of this particular hub arranges itself it is the intention for that recovery consumer to be able to establish their own apartment outside of the Institution and have the benefits of the items that were earned in recovery basically I take home package. Ideally, I would like to see The Hub of institutional reboot facilities. Designed in fashion for mental health consumers and those recovering from drugs and alcohol.

The concept of this institutional Center would be designed for the benefits of the individual needs in order to understand what it takes to be re-established and independent in order to begin a new life and recovery.

Understanding the Vision in order to Create the Potential and then working with what we have available in order to achieve transparencies in these reboot institutions.

I think if the architectural construct in order to build in the way to always have ways to build on, in order to grow the institution as more funds become available.

CONCLUSION

From February 21st of 1997 - To May 30th 2018

I will have concluded a 21-year Mental Health duration of ongoing medical concerns.

I was hospitalized 12 times in Marquette General Hospital and 1 time in War Memorial Hospital throughout this prolonged recovery.

Over the course of this period of time I have been able to establish alongside of my medical team and doctor, a full and successful recovery.

Mental Health Awareness Month of Memorial weekend 2018 will conclude my intensive treatment team care.

I will be moving into regular outpatient appointments.

Through the last 4 years of my recovery I have held Health securities including a recovery with no more symptoms of illness no medical change and no more side effects from the drugs clozapine and lithium.

These Health Securities continued to prove themselves over the last 4 years. I want to keep in mind for the readers that clozapine was a last resort medication, and since every individual has different biological makeups, some medicines may work really well with others and not so much with some, so I want to encourage if you are being medicated for certain symptoms, that there is many uses of Medicine in order to treat all sorts of disorders.

I have been told since I was a youth to have faith in your doctors.

I often would tell myself if God can work in a surgery room then in like manner God is also in the medical fields.

Part of treatment is being able to discuss with your doctor about the symptoms that are present and exhausting those efforts in a way that you are both comfortable, it is okay to get a second opinion if necessary, but we need to continue to Instill the Confidence and Faith in our Medical Teams and Doctor's.

"LIFE IS MADE UP OF ALL THINGS,
ALL THINGS ARE POSSIBLE"
John N. Ruonavaara

Sharing your thoughts about this book by posting a (review online) automatically reaches more and more people. Please post a review to share awareness.

Thank you!

Author, John Ruonavaara

www.ingramcontent.com/pod-product-compliance
Lightning Source LLC
Chambersburg PA
CBHW031226120626
46545CB00003B/1009